May '08

To Gumm...

Paul...

from Mum.

C000071155

This edition published by Ravette Publishing 2007.

ISBN 13: 978-1-84161-284-3

ℛ R
RAVETTE PUBLISHING

I know I'm not
perfect but
I'm so
close
it scares me

Instant human, just add bubbles

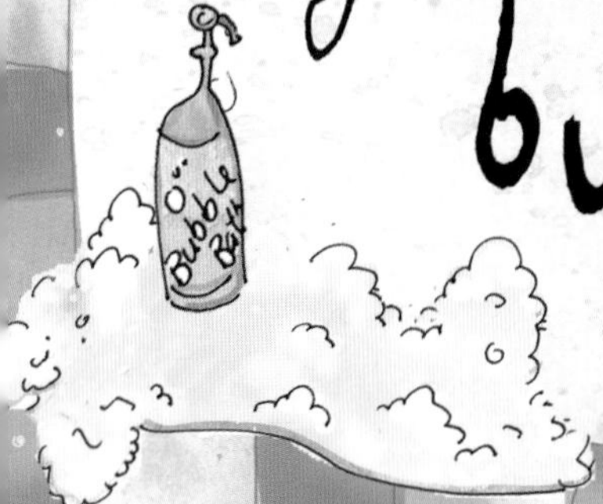

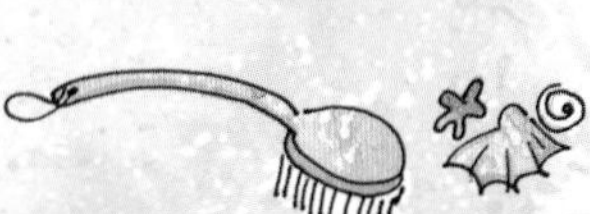

You can't
control everything,
your hair was put on
your head to
remind you
of that

I would be
unstoppable
if I could just get
started

This is **not** the life I ordered

I can only please one person per day. Today is not your day. Tomorrow doesn't look very good either.

The years have been kind, it's the weekends that have done the damage

If you look like your passport photo, you're **not well** enough to **travel**

I knew there would be would be days like this, just not so many

A little less
conversation
a little more
action

I try to watch what I eat but I'm not fast enough

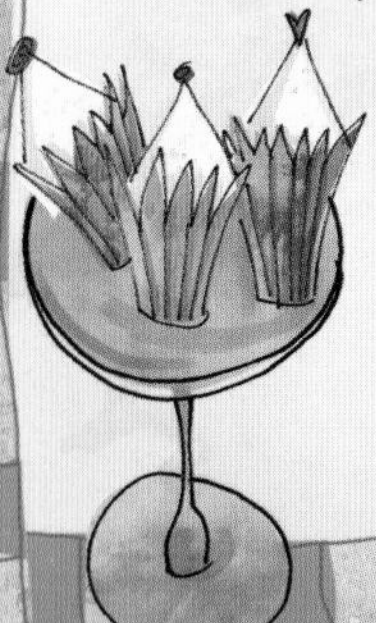

It's all
about
me

I am in **no** shape to exercise

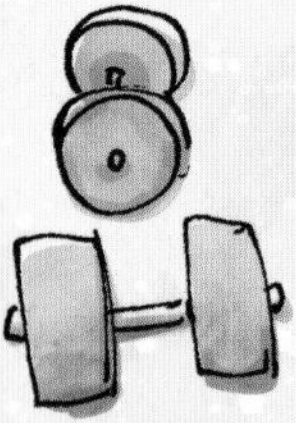

I'm out of bed and dressed... what more do you want?

The years have been kind it's the high heels that have done the damage

Other BORN TO SHOP titles available ...

HOW TO ORDER   Please send a cheque/postal order in £ sterling, made payabl to 'Ravette Publishing' for the cover price of the books and allow the following for post & packaging ...

UK & BFPO   70p for the first book & 40p per book thereafter
Europe & Eire   £1.30 for the first book & 70p per book thereafter
Rest of the world   £2.20 for the first book & £1.10 per book thereafter

RAVETTE PUBLISHING LTD
Unit 3 Tristar Centre, Star Road, Partridge Green, West Sussex RH13 8RA
Tel: 01403 711443   Fax: 01403 711554   Email: ravettepub@aol.com

Prices and availability are subject to change without prior notice.